ICE

ALSO BY DAVID KEPLINGER

POETRY

The Rose Inside
The Clearing
The Prayers of Others
The Most Natural Thing
Another City
The Long Answer: New and Selected Poems
The World to Come

IN TRANSLATION

The World Cut Out with Crooked Scissors: Selected Prose Poems
    (Carsten René Nielsen)
House Inspections (Carsten René Nielsen)
The Art of Topiary (Jan Wagner)
Forty-One Objects (Carsten René Nielsen)

MULTIMEDIA

By & By: The Copybook Songs of Isaac P. Anderson

ICE

poems

DAVID KEPLINGER

MILKWEED EDITIONS

First paperback edition, published 2023 by Milkweed Editions
Printed in the United States
Cover design by Mary Austin Speaker
Cover illustration by Franz Marc, *Birth of the Wolves* (*Geburt der Wölfe*), 1913
23 24 25 26 27   5 4 3 2 1

Library of Congress Cataloging-in-Publication Data

Names: Keplinger, David, 1968- author.
Title: Ice : poems / David Keplinger.
Description: First paperback edition. | Minneapolis, Minnesota : Milkweed Editions, 2023. | Summary: "Ice is an index of findings from the places most buried by time-in permafrost or in memory-and their brutal excavations"-- Provided by publisher.
Identifiers: LCCN 2022049785 (print) | LCCN 2022049786 (ebook) | ISBN 9781639550166 (trade paperback) | ISBN 9781639550173 (ebook)
Classification: LCC PS3561.E5572 I34 2023 (print) | LCC PS3561.E5572 (ebook) | DDC 811/.54--dc23
LC record available at https://lccn.loc.gov/2022049785
LC ebook record available at https://lccn.loc.gov/2022049786

Milkweed Editions is committed to ecological stewardship. We strive to align our book production practices with this principle, and to reduce the impact of our operations in the environment. We are a member of the Green Press Initiative, a nonprofit coalition of publishers, manufacturers, and authors working to protect the world's endangered forests and conserve natural resources. *Ice* was printed on acid-free 100% postconsumer-waste paper by Sheridan Saline.

For Judith Bowles

CONTENTS

I.

II.

III.

ICE

I.

How frozen I became and powerless then . . .
—DANTE, *THE INFERNO*

ICE

"The severed head of the world's first full-sized
Pleistocene wolf was unearthed in the Abyisky
district in the north of Yakutia . . . on the shore of
the Tirekhtyakh River, tributary of Indigirka."

SIBERIAN TIMES, JUNE 26, 2020

What I heard is that the locals searching
for the mammoth tusk along the Tirekhtyakh
discovered instead the head of a wolf
that had been frozen over forty thousand
years ago. The tongue hung from its mouth.
The teeth were terrible but mostly there.
The head alone was the size of a child.
When the local people found the full-grown
wolf head on the Tirekhtyakh and pulled it
like a molar from the sopping gummy earth
and hoisted it, the hardened points of fur
cut through the gloves into their hands.
On each side of the face the eye, sealed shut.
When we read about the story of it together,
those were the days when we would stay up
all winter in the house writing poems in our
icy rooms. You wanted a child. I don't know
where that question got buried in my body.
The wolf head lived on top of its body
in the valley on the river and we cannot know
how the head got severed from the heart.
The body may have dropped and collapsed
into grass roots and larches. Or it may have

been cut from the wolf. But the head stayed
intact, as it still is, as it feels that way now,
the heft and the size of a child. Cocked sideways
in its question on the shoulders of the world.

THE PUPPET TIGER THAT MASCULINITY IS

When I say *tiger*: I mean the catatonic one,
of William Blake, its roar stalled while rising
between the diaphragm and the uvula.
Or I could mean my Daniel, the flattened,
ineffectual puppet tiger of my childhood.
He seemed to lack a mandible: the voice spoke
feebly from outside his body. My father's name
was Daniel. His father's name was Daniel.
In the Neighborhood of Make-Believe they all set out
to find Blake's Tyger once and for all.
It takes them exactly the length of my life
until they come across it among leaves falling
in their eighteenth-century cursive against the sky.

CANTO

Sometimes the luggage spoke to me as I walked half
sunk into the rafters. A satchel complained of money pangs.
The grandfather's steamer knew trees, hammered
under duck cloth, and the fear of the animal that leathered
its surfaces. What it was to travel, they told me.
To be carried down a boulevard of hats, on a gray noon
by the sea, in an overfull century, with bread crammed
into a beaten valise, or in a boat on high waters, and the seagull
that God is, always just there, hanging in one place
for the entire journey. They told me something had filled me, too,
and like them, I'd had no say. After they were emptied, the suitcases
still had nasty dreams of flying open while at sea, and of cities,
the night a galley hold, its buildings stacked together. They knew
the feelings of the earth: round handbag sliding
on the floor of space, also on its voyage somewhere.

ALMOST

A man almost an old man was in my house,
painting walls. The paint, satin white

he stirred with a stick. The work, about
finished, felt heavy in me, a tactile weight

similar to gulping heavy cream. I said
to him *looks like you're wrapping up* to which

he said *almost* and turned to face me.
The paint crept down the wall where

he'd last touched it. That was ten years
ago. I had a friend who made the faces

she witnessed as a war photographer
come alive for others who had no knowledge

of what the war could have been like. One picture
was a child who had no face to speak of.

Many plastic surgeries glommed the
making of an almost-face against

what was his face. My friend stood back
and took the picture. That was her job.

I think of all the work that must be done,
none of which I will have done. It will be

painted over by other work. The hall was bright
and drying when the painter left. The friend

just kind of vanished from my life.
With no known effort I can trace, I am

still here in the same house, touching
with my hand the wall, the hardened

teardrop of the paint where the painter said
almost and turned around to look at me.

NEAR YAKUTIA

Of all the animals   who had their turn
to remind me   this was my doing   I have taken things
without impediment   the oldest was
the rhino   near Yakutia   found in her wool
in August   when the ice roads   became passable

dredged like a galleon   dry-docked   in mud
calloused   as she wrecked   slowly into their hands
then given a name   and a body   and a weight
a portion   of the mass   of the planet hanging
under pounds of gaseous carbon   pluming into air

and she lay   still drowning   in what was once
a riverbed   wet tundra   around the time hands
were inventing   axes, implements of taking   let me
be taken   let me know what falling is   let her thwart
my life   this baby   this whelp   of the herd

who had somewhere to get to   who had somewhere
to get to   who had somewhere   to get to
and propelled herself   like the ship   that passed over Icarus
when the sky   began to clear   as the axman axed
and the ice broke   in pieces   unhanding everything

MY MOTHER REMEMBERS WHAT HAPPENED

Where the action of digging became
her long life, her struggle to know
her own body, its ice of headache,
its ulcer's fire, until she re-
membered herself (this is the craft),
in a chair in the basement, saying
sweetly to us *that was very strange*
when that happened, and her head
looked down to scan her body moving
all together for the first time.

ROCKER

On rainy days she mended the socks of us grandchildren
with her thread

      on its bobbin, and socks of all sizes lay in a basket
like a haul of deflated fish, with holes and frayed ends

instead of scales and gills. The rocker gave the impression of a ship,
                             a journey,

from which there was no escape, her face in the dark unchanging
      when she tested the line as all fishermen do.

IRISES

Whatever is defined by a body must know the heft of receiving gifts, food crammed down the mouth, weight and huge thoughts shoved into one's hands. I am asking how much more I have to learn from this. You are asking that same question. Neither of us says a thing. We are too busy looking at the irises, watching the irises nodding off. How soon they fall across the garden bed, like nails quickly hammered into wood, a little sideways.

LEMMING OF THE ICE AGE

Let us see how specialness

survives past death. The hind legs broken and internal organs
black folds inside. It was a little child

                              who dug it up, cupped it
in her hands and took it home. Like at the exhumation

of the murderer or the saint,
                    some skin has yet to be dissolved.

It is still possible to see the muscle of the wrist and ankle,
but not the head. Now a skull

          with the roots of the smallest
yellow tusks in the world lies exposed. With the jaws that held its squeal

for all this time. With the claws that grew adept
                              at grasping.

ICE MOONS

Ganymede

There is mostly just a film of ice, but just underneath the ice is a saltwater ocean, complete with sea monsters and sunken galleons. Wherever the sea touched rock within the inner mantle, life sprung into form. Ganymede, named after a boy from Troy so beautiful, he was stolen by Zeus and turned into a waiter. Sent away to Mount Olympus, he circles Jupiter with a tray of cold drinks, inside of which still swim Charybdis and Scylla, disguised as two olives run through by a sword.

Europa

It was the craterless, striated world of Europa that Henri Rousseau called up for his famous lion, though the artist didn't know that fact. On the craterless, striated world of Europa, there's so little oxygen, you quickly fall asleep. Therefore, the lion is so quiet, so careful. Because the air is thin, his eyes are these perfect, forced-open orbs. In order to devour whatever he can, he must not lose consciousness. Not yet.

Puck

An idea is getting smaller in God's mind while another grows larger. One constricts; the other, dilated, opens in the dark. On some planets it's the unseen, un-Sun, that shines down—or seems to shine—as if it were a sun. On the moon called Puck, which is able to dodge the ice bullets of Saturn's rings, it is always night like that. Puck moves with confidence and purpose. Same way that sleepwalkers can pass through darkened rooms, aware of all the furniture in front of them.

Ophelia

A globe. Ophelia is a globe, orbiting the globe of Uranus, which orbits the globe of the sun. On Ophelia the dream of Ophelia, invented by a man, is not yet insane with grief, and she is walking on her heels through the fields of mutagenic, hepatotoxic rue, along a river.

Charon

Charon is no moon if Pluto is no planet, the ultimate demotion in rank. But he's set up for life in coin, and his boat very crowded now with nowhere to go, with a hundred billion human souls aboard, anyone who ever lived and died, each with less in common than this bit of space they share, a river cold and quiet on a night flowing backwards, like this one.

SKETCH OF WINGS IN GORHAM'S CAVE

"In a paper published in *Science,* in May, 2010, they introduced what Pääbo has come to refer to as the 'leaky replacement' hypothesis. Before modern humans 'replaced' the Neanderthals, they had sex with them."

ELIZABETH KOLBERT, "SLEEPING WITH THE ENEMY," *THE NEW YORKER*

It may be a name
on the wall of the cave,
this double-winged ace,
this artist's sketch
made by you,
evaporated one,
exterminated
here in Neanderthal City
forty ancient Thebes ago.
It breaks the skin of sediment,
still pumice-soft,
and puts you in the thin line
of my gaze.
As your murderer
and your poor son
I turn in your direction
in my body
and face the portion
of the women assimilated,
the men killed before
their eyes. This is the terrible

meeting of Oedipus
and Laius
in Hell. I excavate your skill
for satisfaction. Decode
the friendly way I brush
at bumblebees. You speak
through me with certain
kinds of touch,
or my ambition
towards a beautiful sameness,
and now and then you might
appear in me at the crossing
where some cobweb shines,
a spindled Andromeda
I duck and go
around. I am sorry
for the parts you gave me
that I've misshapen, turned
into the fawn, a conniving
smile that softens
the points of my sentences.
I bite my fingernails, chew
on the prayer flags of skin.
The wings explode
into a segment of my memory
that was erased—and I don't even try
to follow them.

THE CONGER ICE SHELF HAS COLLAPSED

> "NASA scientist says complete collapse of ice shelf as
> big as Rome during unusually high temperatures is
> 'sign of what might be coming.'"
> *THE GUARDIAN,* MARCH 25, 2022

It must have been a terrible year
of weather for the tongue

of the glacier to collapse like that
the way columns fall in unison

and I am looking at a photograph
when a small portion of the article

at the right-hand corner of my phone
disintegrates around the picture

of a family in winter coats standing
waiting for a bus in rainy weather

that will take them to another border
as the Conger ice shelf collapsed why

did I not hear this commotion
why is every newspaper turning into water

the empire of ice the family in flight
the glacial tongue lolling back into the mouth

of my sleep

SPARTAK THE LION CUB LIVES UNDER
THE PERMAFROST

All signs here indicate that he was real.
Here: yawning, cartoonish, snow-hugged,
flattened on his pillows, under the grave

of ice. Four hundred centuries of mewl,
mewl—and the soul still seems so huge
for both of us, who wish to stay alive.

The sense that some dead mother in the landscape
knows one, that she has licked one's body
clean. Looking at him now, his eyes
closed shut, the fur in cowlicks straight-up

on his back, I know a little bit about
the way it was. I know that there was one
to say without words *there really is no death,*
when he was pressed into this velveteen.

COME AND SEE

Then they stopped coming to the woods

when I walked home as I do tonight

at eight their favorite time to munch the

tart green shrubs that grow wild without

the world's involvement

I wish they could have known me too

as one of their own a deer like them

but in the forest things kept growing

anyway even without the deer without

their bodies parting through the great tableau

and I know that they are absent now

and in their absence I might better understand

who they were or what they meant

to do with the rest of their lives this

is the rest of my life the main road meets me

it is nearly dark I watch the human faces

in the windows of the restaurants the fireman

washes a chrome ladder in the firehouse

as in the twilight I begin to see

what could be called a witness

in the fallen dead branches in the bamboo

however obstinately in the flowers

which even hidden stand and open up

their small green trumpets anyway

TRAVELING

You have told me that at night you travel to a place where spiders rule with scepters made of sewing needles; and you have said: without a body love is limitless. Without I and You. Us and Them. You know this and sometimes wake up clawing the carpet like it's the haunches of your mother, and you have not come back yet as a fully human body—but almost, maybe a lemur.

AT OSIP MANDELSTAM'S MEMORIAL STATUE IN VORONEZH

Now that you've become a statue,
you can be calm. You have made it
to the future. You can raise your giant
muscular hand to your heart,
alleged to be yourself, a man named Osip,

your eyes the size of thank-you notes,
the lids of their green envelopes wet
and unfazed. Now that you're a story,
complete with irreversible choices
and the physics of their consequences,

as lightest rain floats down through
trees in this park like funeral confetti,
you stand here in the permanence of gravel,
with the roses those who never knew you
have scattered in no pattern at your feet.

TWO HORSES IN A FIELD

Is it the speechless speech
that makes their being here
together, unembarrassed, embraced,
fill me with happiness? I want to love

the world like this. I want to say myself
backwards from the room. Even as I ask
this of myself, I am starting
to become myself. The horses stand

in the shape of a T. One of the horses
rests her jaw onto the spine's aging curvature
of the other horse. Not to say

which is the tenderer. The hurt place
is simply where they meet. Their stillness
flawless. The sky a white glove.

THE ICE AGE WOLF THAT LOVE IS

"Dogor [is] an 18,000-year-old pup unearthed in
Siberian permafrost whose name means 'friend' in
the Yakut language."

SMITHSONIAN MAGAZINE, DECEMBER 3, 2019

You'd grown three weeks into your mouthful
of teeth, before your eyes froze shut and then

your throat, but now you are thawing, moping
again, pretending to be tongue and wet fur and

padded feet. My darling whose day has come.
From out of your mother you fell into ice, at play,

in a pocket of snow, pure love that dug deep,
as the mama and the others dissolved quickly

and the father who'd gone to the important place
did not return. It took one night for the world

to harden you into a long bewildered thought
but eighteen thousand years before the ice

like a pipe, like a vein, burst open—until I say
your full name: Dogor, small bulb that keeps

growing new wolf bodies. Dogor, don't harden
your eyes and return to the dead. Dogor, don't

freeze again. Don't fight me or take flight into
a thousand motes of ice. Dogor. Don't bite.

Remember what you are. Leap into my face. Doze
in the crook of my big-boned shoulder. Stay Dogor.

II.

Research is mourning.

—RICK BAROT, *THE GALLEONS*

CHAMELEON

> "The real history of consciousness starts with
> one's first lie."
>
> JOSEPH BRODSKY, *LESS THAN ONE*

To name you is to lie: *came alone*. Part *camel-,*
here is the hump of the backbone. Part *-lion,*
here is the mane down the nape. And to the source
that you have imitated, you are the *shame-loan.*
You may know you have borrowed
what you never gave back, perched on my hand,
a beating, million-year-old mood ring, or poised
like the child with the lasso, the tasseled tongue.
Before you move again across the desert of becoming,
embedded and embodying, I am the target
you've hooped with your gaze: then you drag me back
into the infinite, like a *camera-lens.*

THE FUTURE OF DESIRE

Looping home again
to the year of our affair,
a year I know as broken,
I want you still there.
I imagine that you live
there. I tell you: I didn't love
my body. I would kiss
that year what anything
demanded me to kiss.
That's why our understanding
as you used to call it
has never left the baby fat
of an adolescent memory.
I didn't care for me.

I met you on the dinner
shift at the ice machine.
You told me almost nothing
of who you were before.
A couple years a stripper
and your husband,
drunk, once broke your wrist
clean through the radius,
pulling your hair toward
his purpled face.
I carried all your heavy trays.
I lifted them over my head.
I told you it was easy.
I didn't care for me.

The danger has a way
of making itself a story.
We run false hope
as if it were a red light.
As if it were a red light
and once more in a loop
I suck the vodka taste
of your ice. I know
the flavor of my yes.
You light a smoke
and fit it in my mouth
like the branch of a white
tree, as I turn into a story.
I didn't care for me.

THE NORTH

The old sins, like geezers
    come and go
in the body's cheap hotel.

I am still its busboy
    hiding in the smell
of breezeway linens.

The whole idea
    of the old hotel,
what happened there,

seems to float in place
    by some doge's will.
I walk among diseases

up from the south,
    in summer flapping
blue, parasitic wings.

Why did this memory
    never sink?
Why must I punch

that gray clock again?
    Since then, so many of my bodies
have been condemned,

a tray of dirty dishes
        collapsing in my arms.
The eyes dry up

and wilt.
        Beliefs won't keep.
I have a slight cough.

MIRROR, ON THE NIGHT OF YOUR PASSING

I didn't know
   I looked like that.
I didn't have

a face or a body,
   not even a mouth,
and my two

eyes clotted
   like silence does.
I didn't have

a lot of time
   before the eyes adjusted
and the pupils,

widening to meet
   their need,
dampened

on the hundred
   billion photons
or so left to soak

into the surfaces
   of things.
So I stood

an extra second
in front of
your four-centuries-

old mirror
in the dark.
I didn't know

I had no hands,
no ears and
my hair had gone

so black
it disappeared.
I didn't know

I was a child
all this time,
that the hyacinth

desire is, and the
pomegranate seed
of regret

had been a dream.
Before my features
started fading in,

the mirror
did nothing,
proved nothing

and took no sides.
   The way things
actually are,

what I had been
   one second ago,
had nothing to do with

what I was becoming
   before my own eyes
now.

AMERICAN HISTORY IN MÍSTEK

My chalkboard maps were incorrect. I drew Bethlehem where New York should be. In place of the Empire State Building there was a mill stack and a mustard factory where my father used to work. Instead of the great Delaware River and the crossing from Trenton, I drew the Perkiomen Creek where I caught my first sunfish. It cut my hand with its scales. I lived in America my whole life, I finally admitted, but I know nothing about the place. It was snowing already and still dark. We had a long time to wait before the bell. At the antique shops of Místek, the plunder of a hundred years sat dusty on the shelves. In the mustard factory on the blackboard, my father was warming up his car made of chalk, on a street made of chalk, and I was still a small child sleeping.

WHAT IT COULD BE LIKE TO BE TANYA'S RACING
PIGEON AT THE MOMENT THAT IT TAKES TO AIR

The neck tenses. And the muscles begin
to crane their own way upward, toward
the gray cellar door of the sky. The sky
can only ask if it will come. From below

the ruffled crop, one thought will surface
as an answer, to press against the heavy carapace
of belief. It ripples the skin under the wings.
But what holds this wanting where it is,

is just the bib of Tanya's painted fingernail.
Until the nail, like a real nail, is removed
and this body, made so suddenly of want,
undraping into *having*, knows what to do.

ADAGES FOR DRAGONS

It is still the middle of winter. It is still the nineteen nineties. In Místek I'm still walking, getting my shoes wet in the slush and snow. At my apartment, I thrust the shoehorn into the fat bottom lips of each shoe. I tower over them, slayed, the tongues stuck out. This street is named for the dead puppet master and his contraption dragons made of felt and string. *Trnka* he was called, the *r* a key in my mouth, which I am always turning, trying to make the word spin. All my cracked appliances date back to Communism. It takes time for old stoves and toasters to die. It takes time for one notion to slay, like Saint George did, the notion of another. On their sewn-up leather cheeks my shoes weep white laces all night. They were born in the Bata factory in Zlín. Years from now I will remember them: two small heads at the end of one enormous body, made of the night outside, and its cities like shed scales, which are smoldering.

ELATION

"That I might not become too elated, a thorn in the
flesh was given to me."

2 CORINTHIANS 12:7

When they were finished
barn-building, one of the pieces, part of a beam,
lay in its singleness in a corner of the hayloft,
the light shining on it like a just-born
bastard. This is not to say the piece forgotten
from the finished work was holy, but there was
a heavenly hurt it gave me. It was a common
piece of wood, with two holes for screws,
small eyes to vaguely scrutinize their happiness
now that the work was over. I was so little
but already I desired to bring it home and dress
it up, paint tears into the eyes and feed my baby.
To leave it would have caused me harm.

POMADE

It has been so long since anyone has touched it, the fossil of the child's thumbprint has hardened on the surface of the grease. The can belonged to my grandfather, who scolded us for lathering our faces with hot cream in the barber shop, eating the bubble gum for other children, or kicking over the pail with layers of hair going black to white, the bottom layers so thin, they dissolved in the phosphor glow of florescent light. The child must have found this, too beautiful not to touch. Or this could be my own thumbprint, the child I was, now extinct, half skinny raptor body, half bird who climbed the brickwork to the roof.

SMALL PINK READING GLASSES

American thing,
you are nearly invisible, folded up
like a bow tie, with the grease
of my mother's nose still impressed
on the plastic nubs. How do you
do, metallic drugstore throwaway
which I have deemed important
to keep, more so than her glazed
Japanese vase I remember as muted,
as gray as the glaucomic curtaining,
which, after several rounds of bows,
she stepped behind.

MEMORY, A SNOWFALL

By dinnertime the neighborhood
becomes dismissed of lawns and streets. My father scans it
solemnly. At the window he waves away smoke,
like crumpling air with his fist. It gives the impression
of snowy X-rays I have seen, a luminous skull in slow motion.
My father is a thinning, sleepy man. He turns to me,
about to ask a question. No, he is breathing out smoke.
His mouth has parted.

*

There is soap by the sink where he cleans
himself up: scrubbing, eager strokes.
In after him, I fish for the round
slick cake, black like a carp, and hard to hold. The filthy
water snorts as it gets sucked into the ground.
Like an oracle reading the tea, I study the basin
for obvious signs. The dirt is ribbed inscrutably. Snow hurries
down much harder than before.

*

And after dinnertime the clean long strides
of his shovel and the banks are waves on the
two sides of the wet black macadam, sloping
down to the street. By tomorrow
it will be covered again, and he will come out
again, in gloved hands again, which from my window
will be carving the fin of an enormous black fish
he descends, on top of, in memory.

MY MOTHER READING DICKINSON AT THE END

She didn't call her Emily
or Miss Emily
like almost everyone
who disrespected her,
but "This person."
My mother said
she was beginning to get an idea
where the horses' heads
were turning.
The plumbing needed work.
The roof leaked.
There'd been a sudden change
for the worse, of course,
in her disappearing body
and in every corridor
of that house.
My mother lay in her bed upstairs
with her hands on her chest.
The book was open, face-
down on the table by the lamp
like a sunbather.
This person knew
how to live between
the ticking of the clock, she said.
My mother coughed again.
Little dashes in her sentences.
Much of that time, in fact,

her sleep was interposed
with dashes. Holes and tubes
coursed out into November
and the night.

·EROSION

There was a sandy beach
he built for me
in an aquatic tank
out in the garage
the year we stopped trying
with our summertime trips
to fix things
that got worse.
It was made to look exactly
like Strathmere,
the same lines of jetties
I remember
and at the horizon
a glass plate
that pulsed at regular intervals
as a motorized arm
propelled the waves
to the shore.
Today I am taken
by the whole crazy concept of it
as there were parts
my father planted
to be discovered as I age,
where the beach eroded
and seagulls appeared
pecking for scattered
bits of hard bread,
and a version of myself rose out of the sand
with his toy child; or

a naked couple on the beach
lay silent after an argument; or
an old man buried to the neck
gazed up calmly
at the sky.

POSSESS

Just when the rain opened up, just
now when I heard it like radio static
getting louder on the roof I thought
of how the confusions will be all
I may remember of my life, a few moments of bewilderment
in which I knew what being wild
meant, mounting to the volta, the bolt of
lightning and of how I found my father's
navy yearbook among his best things
in the closet and opening it to a page
at random I saw he had circled in red
the word *possess* and wondered did he
think it was misspelled, or did he want
me to know his mind was taken
at the end and his body and it was not him
saying and doing and doing and saying
things. Or did he mean it as command
to possess myself as I have not come
to do or did he mean something else
I do not understand yet, the red circle
in an oval around the egg of light and
the word all soft bones inside.

AMERICAN THANKSGIVING IN MÍSTEK

When I say *tongue*: I mean *tong*, for reaching and grasping. The Devil's tongue is two-pronged like the snake, and God, who speaks telepathically, has none. God who needn't reach and grasp is tongueless: but the Devil holds hard to meanings and speaks with possessives. I was three before I said a word. Now we sit quietly before the meal, and we understand it perfectly. When I say *tongue* I mean *tank*, rolling on treads round the gutter and the palate of the mouth. When I say *thank*, I mean *take*.

THE OAR

It was what you gave me, spattered with white paint

           on the flat end,
stripped of its finish by the gunwale on the other,

so I took it home that summer
    and stood it in the corner of my study.

I wonder if it would be enough to carry me
if my boat were lost on a river, or the bay.

    I would be carried
anyway, you might have said. You knew how waves

carry little boats
despite their plans. Things travel forward

    when there's nothing to impede them.
Things travel forward

also when there is, against the smack of the current, a voice,
           an oar, to make a difference.

*

So many stories begin with rage.
    Then you know it will be a long story,

and when it is long,
    it will have to move slowly.

I'm not making this up, it's just a fact,
    like it was for Achilles and Medea,

or the way you talked about Tecumseh.
    You should have begun with rage,

but instead
    you left it to your people. You lived

a long time away. What do I call the force
    that propelled your work,

now that there is no mass to carry it?

I'd call it wonder, but no, not that,
    not merely wide-eyed heartfulness.

You bent down to things, hardheaded,
    squinting, wanting to see.

*

I am not amazed
    it has continued on
without you.

Another day
    and I'm amazed
that I'm still here,

still writing
    things down.
You were old

and I was young
    when I met you.
You said

while standing
    in the kitchen
making coffee

not counting
    how many spoons:
the universe had to be,

but it didn't
    have to be beautiful.
The week you died

a deer in winter
   stepped out of
the woods here,

watching me
   watch her
on the grass

next to the road.
   It was dark.
That was back

in January. No headlights
   on the road.
Nothing, at least

in the way the world
   calls action, appeared
to be happening.

THE FIFTEEN-YEAR-OLD DOG SURRENDER IS

Your whole life
you panted after *who-came-here-just-now,*
a bone over there you could smell before
you could see, the wide patch of yard
and a figure of a deer darting in a feral
blur through trees. The joy when some
hand behind you lets go and sends you
running down the open snowy road,
and you are yourself again or for the first
time. Though now what use is there
to tense the metal leash. Now to learn
to work the new trick: one who waits.
It was long ago you learned to run
home. You learned to chase for nothing.
That was the beginning of your training.
That was when the sky was your whole head.
Now to go on. And to go on. To become
the sick hip, the tagged skin, gnawed bone.
To learn the first art with more willingness
and then to sit, lie down.

DRIVING THROUGH KANSAS AT NIGHT

Why must some sorrows go on forever
and follow you from house to house
like the tarnished silverware of ancestors
to whom you owe your life,
or tail you mutedly like this moon

that rules Route 70. Plenty of time now
to think of who is suffering somewhere else,
waking once again to the illness they'll
have to go and look at in the mirror.
Coleman Hawkins plays "Body and Soul"

for the ten millionth time and it is still
good. So it keeps playing on this station
for as long as it stays good, as the cornmills
stream by, small dead empires, and the woman
in the diner gives the signal as you pass.

EMERSON

The outcome, it was said, must be expansion,
more to-ward than re-ward. My grandfather smoked
while cutting hair, his talking mouth tightened
over a cigarette, the floating ashes mechanically
combed away or brushed into oblivion by the batting
of a hand. In the memorable there is always
an acceptance and a resistance at the same time.
Me, I miss the mass in Latin, I miss the censer's
smoky chandelier above my childhood, and the
priest with the ash from cigars puffing words
in the sacristy. To see as a means of being-with. With-
ness as witness. To encounter a mind that startles me,
as Emerson instructed. At the barber shop in dim light,
in the only photograph of my grandfather at my age,
some long-frozen moment in the nineteen thirties,
the customer sits and lets him do the work.
How to hold the beautiful, at the moment of its startling?
To be that barber, to become that customer at the same
time. One must look down and do the work. One must
keep still and watch it all unfolding in the mirror.

III.

Beauty—be not caused—It Is.
—**EMILY DICKINSON**

READING THE LIGHT SURROUNDING THE LARK

> "Buried and frozen in permafrost near the village
> of Belaya Gora in north-eastern Siberia, the bird
> was discovered by local fossil ivory hunters . . . .
> Radiocarbon dating revealed the bird lived around
> 46,000 years ago, and genetic analysis identified it as a
> horned lark."
>
> CNN, FEBRUARY 21, 2020

What you are witnessing
is not merely residue
of ice.

They chiseled it apart
by toothbrush.
For the permafrost

had coated it like plaque.
But it was not a tooth.
It was not

rotten. It was perched
underground
in its negative tree.

It was a lark,
and it has always been
a lark,

then the underground cloud
cracked, melted—
and the lark

fell upward to our world.
To read the light
around the lark, imagine

you have chiseled part
of you away,
an old part at the beginning

of a succession
of your childhood bodies.
You fall upward

from your previous body
out of the melting ice.
And when you look back

on each body,
if you will brush
them carefully,

if you will chisel
what is not you, carefully,
you will know

that each is still bewildered
and desiring to stay
in what it must believe

is the only world, the one
that is safe,
the real one.

READING EMILY DICKINSON IN AMHERST, MASSACHUSETTS

I know how it feels   to live   in a small leaden room,

with only snakes and birds   as consolation. I know how

to imagine death   by falling   through stories

of floorboards   like a poem flutters   through molecules, air

and time. It never lands   in the yard.   The trick

is not to die   while dreaming   of death. That's why

the circle of doors   and windows here   remain open

a little. That's why the poems   seem often to end

on slant rhymes, and dashes. That's why   the hawthorn cone

is never quite   in full bloom   but almost. I too   come here

respectfully. I bow, halfway   at thresholds.   I know how to wait

at a completely empty window,   holding out my hands.

READING *GILGAMESH* BEFORE GOING TO SLEEP

In some dreams it is possible to visit Uruk and to be its king
as I did sensing all along I was a bad king predisposed
to impatience and affronted by impertinence and I know now
what I really needed was a good friend who could teach me things

Yes that is what happened as I fell asleep with my arm
on the barrel-chested dog prone to snoring and standing straight up
on the bed at night or barking at the snap of thunder or a neighbor slamming
his fist into a wall I have known all along I am my own bad friend

but we have killed the monster loneliness and though injured
with a bum leg and then the hips and then the kidneys failing
the dog kept showing me what I am not how I am not like her
not uncomplaining not joyful in a time of joy not querulous at things unseen

not guarded in a time of danger and when she left I walked through oceans
of myself
like Gilgamesh searching for a way to stay in pain forever
because I didn't know how else to honor what had died for me
—Yes I was wrong of course I was an idiot a king of human beings

and when I had the chance to live I was distracted anyway—
Then it was possible to see the rheumy-eyed and coughing old
citizens of my city and to weep for what I should have known
that I was the rheumy-eyed and coughing citizen dying which is the only way
to visit Uruk and to become its king

READING THE BUFFALO'S FACE

Moving along we went to the dairy farm
where they also had goats and horses and one
very old, very slow, American buffalo.
I think

it's long gone now, I think it's moved along, too,
to its pedestal, staring no less evenly at children
with their ice cream from its shamble
of a face.

The fur hung like a shredded hood thrown over
what seemed an insupportable skull. My father
leaned down to say the herds once flourished
thousands of miles

from here. I stood high on a step. I could see
the buffalo directly, the one eye, not moving,
that face a book too big for me, its opened page
that smelled of earth.

READING JAKE'S POEMS AT THE SOUTHERNMOST POINT

All day the beautiful hunters are trying to get fed, and at the moment
　　they see *shine*

the pelicans dive and come up with the gular pouches mostly empty
　　except for water, salt,

and air. This is what they are, this is how they must go on, grammatical
　　brackets at a distance,

just off the key where the ocean folds over and over, sealing incrementally
　　smaller envelopes of itself,

in what must seem a correspondence whose content diminishes until it
　　recedes back to its source,

erasing everything. Today, light wind, come far from the Dry Tortugas.
　　I think of that affection

you held onto for the hymnal word, *abide*. The feeling of the word in the
　　mouth, my mouth

as I speak it. What abides? Surely something must burst out beyond itself,
　　even now,

even what is taken, lifted into brackets at a distance, at the moment
　　it began to shine.

AT THE MUSEUM OF THE SCALPEL AND THE EAR HORN

1. *The Short French Verse of Rilke*

At the end he wrote less frequently in German
until he had to salvage what was left by packing it
quickly into a suitcase: a small valise
containing the one word, *absence.*

2. *Removal of the Small Parts of the Body*
"What a falling off there was . . ."
        HAMLET

A sequence of incidents starting with
a tooth my Rosencrantz
a polyp my Guildenstern
to the greater organs in order of importance
eventually leading to the actual disease
and after that, the silence.

3. The Invisible Man *by H. G. Wells*

It never describes the obvious,
which is the most ghastly part,
which is the moment when the man
is naked and unbandaged and invisible
alone in a room thinking nothing,
touching nothing, saying not a word.

4. The Unknown Musical Career of Emily Dickinson

The piano had no sustain pedal,
so whatever note she played
ended with the touch of a finger
to the keys

and erased itself, while against
the convolutions of that brain
the musical staff allowed for this,
allowed for this

enormously long composition
hanging slanted in the air, always
a whole note one moment in length,
then nothing.

5. Lena Horne in Glory

A hundred years from now someone will lilt
their voice just so, singing, *can't go on,*
closing the glottis of the true vocal folds,
diminishing, finishing the note, and it will be you
they will be honoring, though they won't know it
by the shape of the air they make tremble, like you
made air tremble.

6. In the Language of the Dead

Eventually you stopped
coming to me

except when I would hear
in my head

the words of the language
only you and I could speak

a kind of baby tongue
that looked at things

and said with surprise
their names

missing tooth
yeast soup

nonpareil

ASSEMBLING THE BONES INTO THE BODY OF
THE SAINT

At every visit it was snowing on the dead lakes
at the home of the mystic Roche de Coppens
a saint a very large man who'd broken his back
on a motorcycle and claimed to have healed himself
by some invention
he called prayer

I believed him I saw it myself he could walk and often
stood and stretched out his arms in a yawn
that's how he mounted the bones
that's how he healed himself continually daily repeating
but when I read the notes later I could not understand
my own words

Roche de Coppens I ask the hieroglyphic notebook
I ask the silence today is there a point to all this singing
are you there are you still there and right away in my head
out of the snow of confusion there comes some equally
baffling answer in the voice of a large man yawning saying
gorgeous things
like *yes*

AT THE MUSEUM OF SUPERNATURAL HISTORY

The guide said there was more to see, as if to apologize, and we
had better
heed the time.

              So we all made the correction
on our watches as we went on to the next item

and a long night ahead of learning the atomic weight
of thought, the velocity of spit, the average IQ of stones,

              the telephone
number of every mirror in every house in the world
                            we'd never lay eyes on again.

READING JAMES WRIGHT IN MARTINS FERRY, OHIO

Near Steubenville
in Martins Ferry
and the dried-up
football fields
he only saw again in memory,
on a Saturday Annie Wright
spoke in the public library
of the summers in Fano
where they got well.

The work,
Annie said, made this space in Jim
for an Italian amphitheater
of the mind,
and Li-Young read the late poem
for the hermit crab.

It wasn't nostalgic then,
and it isn't today, the loneliness.
But I find the language
heavy with a struggle
that has calcified now.
Underneath the shell, every tender animal
seeks a way to stay alive.

Who doesn't feel that.
I felt that.
The old librarian,
nodding off, felt that.

The grass on the football fields burning
and the hermit crab,
bulging in the house
it has to leave again,
must feel that,
too.

GHAZAL

All around on the street I kept finding David. I saw the heart on its own still working for David, outside his body, beating itself, the deviant muscles worn down, flattened, like old seats in a theater. I tried to force it back inside David. I found a line of trees that led into the daydream of his life, the parts of David I didn't know existed, and plucked a little David yet to bloom. Do not put me in your mouth, it said to me.

READING LIGHT

What a small room
  my father said
when he would press

the old door open
  warped in January
and cast his eyes on me

after bedtime what
  an incredibly small room
the buzzing reading light

lengthening me
  prematurely
my head in dark relief

on the backboard
  of the monastic bed
those winters of childhood

when our twentieth century
  snows fell deep
and my father

would shovel for a half an hour
  a narrow pathway out
and scrape his iced windows

as he ran the telephone truck
    some loose belt screaming
in the hood what

a small room this is
    me half reading half
listening but I knew

my life had what it needed there
    my love of little books
and warm enclosures

and our strange agreement
    about this statement
though I offered nothing

beyond that punctuated click
    when he would close the door and leave me there
the way it was

A HOLLYHOCK THAT ONCE BELONGED TO
STANLEY KUNITZ

Later that week   I found it in my right side
pocket. It had begun   to bloom, blue.   Tissue thin.

To the bottle   of carbolic acid   went your father.
To brain plaque,   the weed   of forgetfulness,   .

went your mother.   Still you felt   a fondness
for the natural thing,   you loved   even the mulch,

and the flower   of the mallow family, hollyhock.
Come in, you said.   From one specimen   of the garden

you cut me   a sprig,   which I pocketed. Taken
from light,   from you, from   its princedom, a small

Gautama.   Then I forgot   it was there, down
there in the dark, doing   its precise work anyway.

THE LAST READER OF THE POEMS

They closed the book on *the stork has gone,* and as the pages folded over the small houses of the words, inside the houses of the words small people stayed up late into the night, writing letters. Like animals sunk into ice, words remain lit inside dead books, without air or time or the eyes that once passed over them. But every gaze was one full day to them. Every reader was a sun.

THE LONG ANSWER

It's now so late,
   the two men
seated in the middle

of the frozen escalator
   on Connecticut Avenue,
underground,

can take their time
   to weld the one
thing to another

thing, anonymous
   and slow. Their heads
almost touch. The sun-

surface flash of the rod
   is not to be gazed into.
In their masks

they resemble
   the gods without names
as under their stairs

I see a small hatch
   has been opened
where the guts

of the moving tread-
   mill are exposed.
They say nothing

to each other. They
   stare down at the work
of making things

work. They will not even
   show their surprise
when the slats,

one folding out
   of the next, begin
to rise as steps

that they will open
   to us, that we will ride
into the open dome

and the summer,
   like the answer
to a question

so old, no one
   can say what was asked
in the first place:

and which leaves
   us, on the tip of
night's tongue,

sleepy and arriving
    in waves of heat,
with only each other,

on Connecticut
    Avenue, come out
from underground.

IS

Now that I see its gorgeous consolations,

its hard math, its equals sign that conjures

metaphor of anything, I know the long life

of the word, transplanted into other tongues,

its cognates disseminated like eyes, and I love

the rhyme's surprise. Let there come a calm

agreement among strangers, saying nothing,

riding in a train. This is. Let there come

the apodictic hush of *esse*. There is an order

that demands I change. Now, nevertheless,

whatever is, will be frozen as a photograph.

It survives from *eom* to *am*, freckled like the egg

in each retelling, each iteration, each unique,

a Buddha's smile, each syllable an iron nail.

I know the troubles of the word: its passive

accusations; *mistakes were made*; how *Is* and *Was*

are the first sparring gods. But it has priestesses

and priests. Beloved, you are one. And I am one.

Let curiosity be prayer. Let being be the rebel

that I frond and crucify. And come to life again.

Lest I be quiet. I rub ashes on my body. I steal fire.

I give you fire. I lower my head.

SONNET

"You are that which is not."

CATHERINE OF SIENA

The stork has gone. Here is the nest.
It teeters on the station tower
like a satellite dish encircled in grass,
or tiny bits of hair, over and over,

or yarn around a pair of unseen hands.
Old transmissions have come to a hush.
The air is static whorl. The road wends.
I wonder at this craft; this bulrush

basket; mouth-in-waiting for its tooth.
The stork was here. Here is the nest.
Praise the giving way, the taking wing.

Praise the singing bowl after the song.
Praise who cast, from such delicate
bronze, an absence.

NOTES

Climate change has so altered the ecosystem of Siberia's Yakutia (Sakha Republic) region, several animal species as old as fifty thousand years have been recovered with their interior organs, fur, teeth, tongues, and other tissue intact. The species named in this collection are merely a few of the proliferation of discoveries that—while they improve our sense of what the planet was like during and just before the last Ice Age—are sobering indicators of unprecedented change brought about by the domination of *Homo sapiens* within the so-called Anthropocene.

The epigraph to part one comes from the final canto of *The Inferno,* where Dante-poet meets Satan impacted in ice at the bottom of the ninth circle. As Columbia University's *Digital Dante* and the breathtaking, expansive *Commento Baroliniano* puts it, "the anti-spiration of un-love freezes the icy core of the universe."

Chart of moons in "Ice Moons": *Ganymede:* One of the four moons of Jupiter, first discovered by Galileo in 1610. *Europa:* Another of the four moons of Jupiter. *Puck*: one of the "literary moons" orbiting Uranus. *Ophelia*: orbiting Uranus. *Charon:* orbiting Pluto, which was declassified as a planet upon the discovery of the dwarf planet Eris, a trans-Neptunian object as large as Pluto is.

"The Oar" is for Mary Oliver.

"Reading Jake's Poems . . ." is for Jake Adam York.

ACKNOWLEDGMENTS

My thanks to the following journals in which earlier versions of these poems first appeared:

AGNI: "Memory, a Snowfall" (parts 1 & 2)

American Literary Review: "Come and See"

Aquifer: "The Fifteen-Year-Old Dog Surrender Is," "A Hollyhock That Once Belonged to Stanley Kunitz"

Copper Nickel: "Adages for Dragons"

Dappled Things: "Two Horses in a Field"

Los Angeles Review: "At Osip Mandelstam's Memorial Statue in Voronezh," "Driving through Kansas at Night," "At the Museum of the Scalpel and the Ear Horn"

New England Review: "Is"

The New Republic: "The Puppet Tiger Masculinity Is"

North Dakota Quarterly: "Near Yakutia"

Poetry Society of America: "Reading Emily Dickinson in Amherst, Massachusetts"

The Moth (Ireland): "Reading Jake's Poems at the Southernmost Point"

Ploughshares: "Reading *Gilgamesh* before Going to Sleep"

Plume: "Pomade"

West Branch: "The North," "The Future of Desire"

"The Long Answer" and "Sonnet" were first included in *The Long Answer*. "Reading Emily Dickinson . . ." was selected for the 2020 Emily Dickinson Prize from the Poetry Society of America.

For their pitch-perfect readings of drafts and revisions and individual poems, my gratitude and awe go out to Sibylle Baier, Jericho Brown, Lorraine Coulter, Henry Crawford, Blas Falconer, Stephanie Grant, Laura Reece Hogan, Mark Irwin, Carsten René Nielsen, Carrie Hannigan, Juan J. Morales, Laren McClung, Jenny Molberg, Majda Gama, Danny Lawless, Katherine Larson, Shawn Parell, Roberta Rubenstein, Sandra Beasely, Kyle Dargan, Patty Park, Dolen Perkins-Valdez, Melissa Scholes-Young, Kathleen Smith, Rachel Louise Snyder, Ilya Kaminsky, Leah Johnson, Wayne Miller, Bill Varner, Linda Voris, William Waltz, Parker Palmer, Joanna Macy, and Adam Tamashasky. Thank you to my wonderful colleagues at American University in the Department of Literature and to all those who have supported me there for sixteen years. Gratitude to Celeste Young, and Zoe Zohs; and to Cathy Schaeff for leading weekly meditations on Zoom; and to my beloved pod, Bobbi Whalen, Dori Sless, Dave Sless, Kermit Moyer, and Amy Gussack, thank you for sanctuary during the pandemic, and to my sister, Dana Meals, and Laura Denardis and Deb Smith for the same. Thank you to Daniel Slager, Lauren Langston Klein, and Tijqua Daiker for their editorial support at Milkweed. To all my family, friends, and peers, living and late: to know you is to feel worthy, to touch the earth.

DAVID KEPLINGER is the author of eight books of poetry, including *The World to Come* and *Another City*, which was awarded the 2019 UNT Rilke Prize. In 2020 he was selected for the Emily Dickinson Award from the Poetry Society of America. His translations include German poet Jan Wagner's *The Art of Topiary*; his translation of Danish poet Carsten René Nielsen's *Forty-One Objects* was a finalist for the 2020 National Translation Award. His poetry has been awarded the T. S. Eliot Prize, the C.P. Cavafy Poetry Prize, the Colorado Book Award, two fellowships from the National Endowment for the Arts, and a Lannan Foundation grant for literary translation. He lives in Washington, D.C., and teaches in the Department of Literature at American University.

milkweed
EDITIONS

Founded as a nonprofit organization in 1980, Milkweed Editions is an independent publisher. Our mission is to identify, nurture, and publish transformative literature, and build an engaged community around it.

Milkweed Editions is based in Bdé Óta Othúŋwe (Minneapolis) within Mní Sota Makhóče, the traditional homeland of the Dakhóta people. Residing here since time immemorial, Dakhóta people still call Mní Sota Makhóče home, with four federally recognized Dakhóta nations and many more Dakhóta people residing in what is now the state of Minnesota. Due to continued legacies of colonization, genocide, and forced removal, generations of Dakhóta people remain disenfranchised from their traditional homeland. Presently, Mní Sota Makhóče has become a refuge and home for many Indigenous nations and peoples, including seven federally recognized Ojibwe nations. We humbly encourage our readers to reflect upon the historical legacies held in the lands they occupy.

milkweed.org

Milkweed Editions, an independent nonprofit publisher, gratefully acknowledges sustaining support from our Board of Directors; the Alan B. Slifka Foundation and its president, Riva Ariella Ritvo-Slifka; the Amazon Literary Partnership; the Ballard Spahr Foundation; *Copper Nickel*; the McKnight Foundation; the National Endowment for the Arts; the National Poetry Series; and other generous contributions from foundations, corporations, and individuals. Also, this activity is made possible by the voters of Minnesota through a Minnesota State Arts Board Operating Support grant, thanks to a legislative appropriation from the arts and cultural heritage fund. For a full listing of Milkweed Editions supporters, please visit milkweed.org.

Interior design by Tijqua Daiker
Typeset in Arno

Arno was designed by Robert Slimbach. Slimbach named this typeface
after the river that runs through Florence, Italy. Arno draws inspiration
from a variety of typefaces created during the Italian Renaissance;
its italics were inspired by the calligraphy and printing
of Ludovico degli Arrighi.